THIS CLASS CAN SAVE THE PLANET

Be a Good Human Co
Books for thoughtful and socially-conscious kids.
BeAGoodHuman.Co

Printed in the United States of America.

ISBN 978-1-7366934-2-1

Library of Congress Control Number: 2021933717

For Roland and Linda, who never wasted anything and made the most of everything they had. -ST

For Pat and Greg, who taught me how to approach the world with kindness. -KB

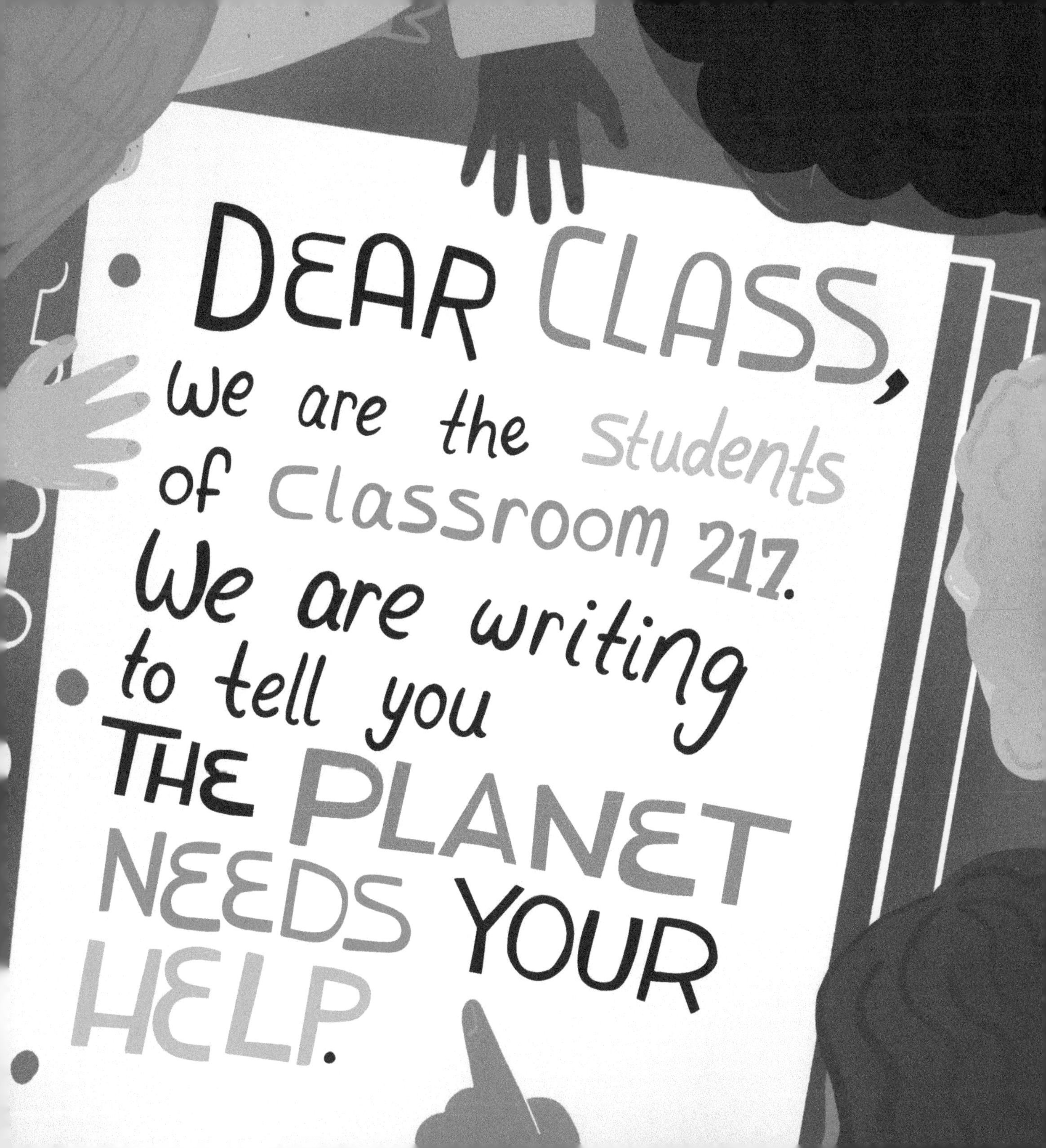
DEAR CLASS,
We are the Students
of Classroom 217.
We are writing
to tell you
THE PLANET
NEEDS YOUR
HELP.

WE CAN ALL
TAKE BETTER CARE
OF OUR OCEANS
AND RIVERS,
MOUNTAINS AND
BEACHES,

THIS CAN FEEL BIG.

AND A LOT TO THINK ABOUT.

AND REALLY HARD AT TIMES.

BUT WE BELIEVE THIS CLASS...

THIS CLASS CAN SAVE PLANET.

will you join us?

INSTEAD OF

USING ONLY ONE
SIDE OF THE
PAPER,

WE CAN
USE BOTH SIDES AND RECYCLE WHEN WE'RE DONE.

When you recycle a stack of NEWSPAPERS just 3 feet high, it saves **1** TREE!

-JJ

RECYCLE HERE!

PLANET

INSTEAD OF

LUNCHES PACKED WITH PLASTIC,

WE CAN CHOOSE REUSABLE MATERIALS

INSTEAD OF THROWING FOOD AWAY, WE CAN

About **HALF** of all food in America is wasted. If we compost it, we could have **HEALTHY** Soil to grow more food!

—Zari

EAT IT,

COMPOST IT.

SAVE IT,

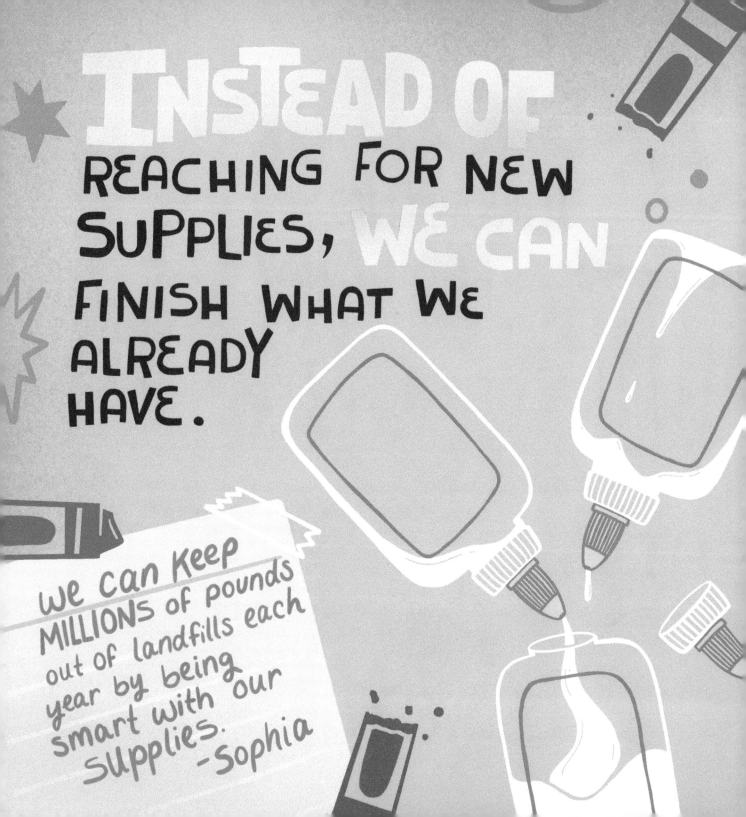

INSTEAD OF TOSSING BROKEN THINGS, WE CAN LOOK FOR WAYS TO FIX THEM.

Used clothes save BILLIONS of gallons of water and keep MILLIONS of pounds out of landfills.
—Liam

INSTEAD OF
THROWING OUT TOO-SMALL CLOTHES,

WE CAN
DONATE TO OTHERS.

COAT AND MITTEN
— DRIVE —

INSTEAD OF BUYING EVERYTHING NEW,

SLIME RECIPE
1 CUP GLUE

1-2 TABLESPOONS SALINE SOLUTION

1 TABLESPOON BAKING SODA

Food COLORING

—Nadia

MAKE PAINT from DRY MARKERS
1. Sort your own markers and gather the ones that don't work.
2. Place markers tip down in cups with a small amount of water. Leave overnight.
3. Remove the markers—RECYCLE.
4. Then use the paint.

—Malik

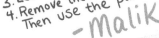

INSTEAD OF KEEPING LIGHTS AND ELECTRONICS ON,

WE CAN POWER THEM DOWN WHEN THEY'RE NOT IN USE.

INSTEAD OF WATER BOTTLES YOU CAN ONLY USE ONCE,

WE CAN SWITCH TO REUSABLE.

Recycled plastic bottles can be made into t-shirts, sleeping bags, and even shoes! — Kiki

INSTEAD OF

BEING SILENT,

WE CAN SPEAK UP AND BE A VOICE FOR CHANGE.

BECAUSE WITH
VOICE AND
ACTION

REDUCE
REUSE
RECYCLE

WE CAN DO
HARD THINGS,
ACHIEVE A LOT,
AND MAKE A
BIG IMPACT.

THE PLANET NEEDS YOU.

IT NEEDS ALL OF US.

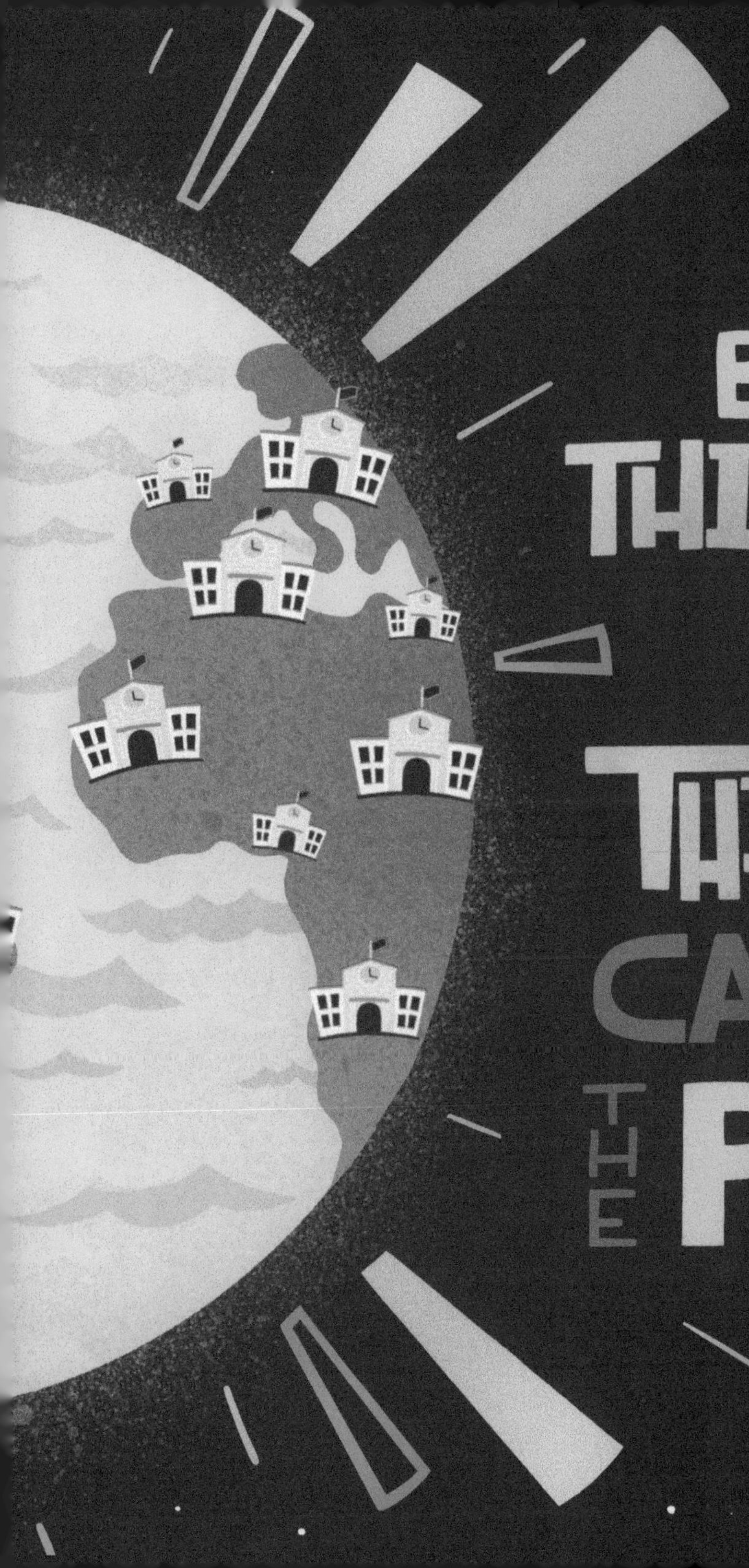

BECAUSE THIS CLASS...

THIS CLASS CAN SAVE THE PLANET.

OUR CLASSROOM GOALS:

SIGN HERE:

ABOUT THE BOOK

We created this book specifically for teachers and students who want to make a positive impact on the environment. We believe students have an incredible ability to change our planet's future for the better.

Stacy's mom, Linda, was a huge influence for this book. She recently retired after spending more than 30 years as an elementary and junior high teacher. During that time, she naturally instilled green and eco-friendly practices in her classroom.

GET OUR FREE CLASSROOM KIT FOR THIS BOOK, WHICH INCLUDES WORKSHEETS, A POSTER, AND COLORING PAGES.

BeAGoodHuman.Co/Save-the-Planet-Classroom-Kit

Stacy Tornio is an award-winning author of many books, including *The Ultimate Book of Scavenger Hunts* and *101 Outdoors Adventures to Have Before You Grow Up*, which she wrote with her son. Stacy lives in Milwaukee, Wisconsin

Kristen Brittain is an illustrator, designer, an lettering artist. You car find her work all over the country on posters, t-shirts, cups, and even socks. Kristen lives in Boston, Massachusetts See more of her work a KristenBrittain.com.

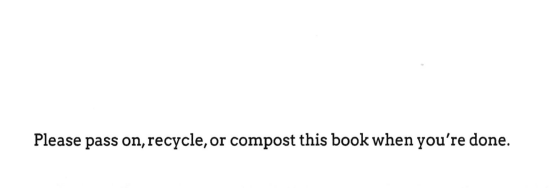

Please pass on, recycle, or compost this book when you're done.

CPSIA information can be obtained
at www.ICGtesting.com
Printed in the USA
BVHW060857150222
629067BV00006B/506